Dear, Nobody...

By Johnny Macarter

Journal entry from early 2020
(during the Pandemic)

I really don't know where this is going; I just know that I am really sad and I hope this helps. I also know that I need counseling to start digging through my childhood trauma. Yesterday someone asked me If I had dealt with my trauma. I thought I had, well atleast come to terms with it. But the more we talked the more I felt the weight of all those burdens come over me. This makes me sad because it's an unknown war for me. I don't know how I will respond to digging up trauma that has been buried for years. I don't know if I will be able to handle it. I don't know If I will go through another depression….alone.

I'm usually pretty strong when it comes to this kinda stuff but mostly because I've become pretty good at burying it and putting it off for as long as I can. But you never truly know how you will respond to something until it happens to you.

I could be overthinking it, I do that…Having a problem doesn't scare me because I'm pretty good at problem solving, but not having a solution to a problem, does scare me. But I guess that's normal right!?

It feels like there are a lot of little fires, some may not be real, some may be linked to another...where do I even start?

Dear, Nobody

You were supposed to be my first best friend, my first teacher & my first true love. But instead you were my first broken heart, my first bully & my first enemy. You made me cold before the world ever could. I constantly felt like I was under attack around you. I always felt that I had to be guarded or completely out of the way. There was never any affection shown, but I guess at that point it wouldn't have made it any better.

I always felt uneasy or unwelcomed in your space. And as a child very little is explained to you so I perceived that as you did not like me or hated me even. We never saw eye to eye on anything. I felt like I got beaten for no reason most of the time.
I wasn't a "bad" kid.

I've always been pretty self sufficient and just kinda did my own thing. It could have been a survival skill though because you never really supported anything that I showed interest in. maybe a small bit of verbal encouragement but nothing that required real effort. And there were so many opportunities; I have alway been a busy person with my hands in a little of everything. School dances, roller blading, basketball, football, weightlifting, dancing etc. you never once said pick something and I'll help you see it through. While being present you managed to be very absent in my entire life, my entire evolution.

I have no core values that I can attribute to you. I learned more of what not to do and how not to treat people so that they don't feel the way I felt. I know that I played my part as well by arguing back and allowing myself to be triggered but I was a kid, you were the adult. You could have done more. At Least that's what I expected. Even now as an adult, not much has changed. But now that I am an adult I understand that you were created with your own purpose, as was I. I understand that while I may have felt that you were indebted to me you had many other purposes in this lifetime that also needed to be fulfilled.

I understand that everything happens for a reason and that everything I went through was for a greater purpose and it made me who I am today. While I'm not perfect I love who I've become despite everything that I've been through that didn't break me. I also understand that a person can only teach you as much as they know and I chose an unfamiliar path to you. So to expect guidance in that space is somewhat unrealistic. And I'm in no way giving you an out for your behavior because I'm big on accountability no matter who you are.

You also hid very vital information from me that I needed so that I could understand myself better, where I came from and part of why I am who I am. And for that reason I will always feel incomplete. I'm just now, at 28, finding out that the man that I have called "Dad" for 28 years is not my biological father. The icing on the cake is that you "had an idea" that he may not have been my biological father but failed to mention it to me at any point over the course of 28 years.

I figured it out on my own while doing an AncestryDna test simply to find out what parts of Africa my lineage came from. And to add insult to injury It linked me to a brother whom I knew, then realizing that not only did I know my biological father growing up just by a different title, but that he had passed away some years ago. I'll never get to have a father/son conversation with him let alone have a relationship with him. You played a major part in taking something so invaluable away from me that I still don't know how I feel about it.

Did you ever think about how I would feel if I ever found out? Did you ever think about how this might affect me?

No, you couldn't have....

We are now in a place where you tell me that you love me, but this doesn't feel like love...**It never has.**

Dear, Nobody

I really don't want to be angry with you, but of all the emotions I feel toward you right now that Is the only one that is clear. I want to believe that you had good intentions when you came into my life but your actions everyday since, contradict that belief. And if we're being honest what you did was f***ked up, selfish and dishonorable to say the least. Why would you rush to sign a birth certificate if you knew that you might not be the father? I personally think you did it for your mother. To please her. And I don't fault her at all. Even if that is the case, she did what was supposed to be done and never questioned it from what I could tell. That's noble. My Issue is honestly not what you did because I'm a very understanding guy, my issue is that you took me away from my father only for you not to step up. That's how I know you didn't do it for you. I have watched you bend over backwards for people and want to help everyone and their mother all my life but you never did that when it came to me. Is that because you knew in the back of your head that we did not share the same blood? Did you notice we did not have similar features? Is that why you were and are still telling people you don't think we're blood related? When were you going to tell me? From my understanding you have been talking about this for a decade at least. So why didn't you tell me? why??

Saying you did the bare minimum is being optimistic. You always showed me love whenever I was in your presence but it was never on your account. It was always because your mom took the initiative and still had to make you come to the house that was roughly 100 feet away from yours.

I know you have your own trials and missions in life and life is hard for everyone rather it be physically or mentally. Your mother was the best thing that ever happened to me so I don't regret how my life turned out. I'm proud of the man that I have become and I owe most of that to her. But I need you to understand how your decisions affected me. I basically grew up without a father. I saw you like every other month if I was lucky. You missed most of my birthdays, school events, puberty, losing my virginity, first heartbreak etc.

And I remember asking myself "If he loves me so much why would he just leave me here?" You often tell me that I'm the best thing that ever happened to you and that you're so proud of me..that sounds like someone you would make a priority. That sounds like someone you really know and love..but who am I? What do you really know about me? Because you've missed it all and you're still missing it. We still only talk once briefly every few months.

For the record I do love you and I do appreciate the moments that we have shared and will share. I do not think you are a bad person, I can say that I know you generally have good intentions for most of your decisions but that doesn't make them right nor does it mean I have to agree with them or respect them. As much as I'm trying not to be, I am still very angry. I'm still trying to rationalize all of this so that I can find a way to forgive you. I don't want to be angry and bitter or hold a grudge with anyone. I've come too far and fought too hard to overcome that version of me that I created to survive an environment that y'all created. I've grown so much and I won't allow myself to be set back by anyone. So one day I will be able to forgive you but unfortunately,

it won't be today.

Dear, Nobody

Hey….I wish this could have been a 2 way conversation but god had other plans. Maybe your purpose in my life was just to give me life to get me here. God took care of the rest I see. I'd like to think that you check in from time to time to see that I'm doing well and that I'm ok. For the record I'm not angry with you. I understand your position in all of this. It was made clear to me that you tried and that you always knew. I do wonder though why you never said anything!? I guess it wasn't really your secret to tell and it would have been a bigger mess. But It was partially your secret as well. I understand that times were different then, your hands were tied legally, and after you tried and tried to get through to her you just stopped. You had feelings too. As a child I never could pinpoint why your energy towards me was off but now it makes sense of course. I just thought you didn't like me because you didn't like him. Which I'm sure had a little to do with it. It's ok, you were human. It's so crazy because I have always felt out of place, Like something was off, never feeling like I belonged anywhere I was but I thought maybe I was overthinking it.

Which Is why I did the ancestry thing in the first place. I just got more than what I bargained for. And now I have a million questions and no answers. I'm a brain picker. I have questions for everything lol like when did you move to the U.S? Why? How long has your family been settled in Jamaica? What is your family like? What are you like? Can you teach me how to make a good Curry chicken roti? That's my favorite dish so far. What were you like as a boy?

How was it growing up in Jamaica? When are you going back? Can I come? And so many more. The idea of that conversation makes me smile. I have been wanting to know more about my roots since high school and now I have to embark on this journey alone. This was supposed to be our journey. Maybe I will form a bond with your kids. Time will tell. I will make an effort though lol If you know nothing else about me know that I do not force myself on people. I'm a pretty good guy so everyone takes to me rather easily.

I do worry though that because so much time has passed that they won't be so welcoming. And with you not being here to oversee the children they may act like, well children. But I expect there to be a little bit of resistance anyway. Respectfully. Considering you are not here to tell your side of the story and confirm my "Alligations" lol but honestly, knowing the truth is good enough for me. Life is good for the most part. That's all I ever wanted. A healthy family dynamic clearly wasn't in the cards for me. But like I said everything happens for a reason and there is comfort in knowing that. For me, anyway.

I'm glad we had this talk lol until next time. See you on the other side.
Things will be different...I hope.

Dear, Nobody

Hey you, We haven't talked in a while. But I'm sure you have been watching my every move and guiding me. Lol You were the only one that I ever felt had my best interest in this world. You always put my needs before yours and for that I am forever grateful. You showed up for me when you didn't have to. You may not have known but you never questioned it either. You loved me unconditionally and that is rare in this world. Rare. It's actually very ghetto down here. It honestly makes me not want to have kids. Especially considering they won't get to meet you. Even when times were hard you made every birthday, holiday and even weekend visits feel special. You even preserved the "Santa is real" concept for as long as you could, even though people spoiled it for us. You tried to protect our innocence. I really appreciated that.

You knew how much I loved seafood so for like 3 birthdays straight you had seafood boils at my birthday party. You were always the one to pay attention to me and took the time to understand who I was. You always knew when something was off with me. You knew things were off at home but it wasn't much you could do. That's probably why you didn't mind getting me every weekend. I hated leaving my friends in the neighborhood but I always had fun once I got to your house. And you would always let our friends and family stay over so we would have friends to play with. You never really let us stay at other people's houses. I didn't understand it as a kid but now I do and I'm so grateful. That was just you looking out for us again.

We had a lot of good times. Hunting, fishing, motorsports etc. were life skills that I'm glad I got. I'm now realizing how invaluable that is. I wish I would have invested more time into it so that I could pass it down. Which I know you would say I still can, and I will. When I tell people that I knew how to pick bones out of fish at the age of 2 they never believe me. Lol I used to love going fishing with Tony. coming home and cleaning the fish together. Real country boy stuff lol I remember we begged for Bb guns for christmas one year. We saw boxes under the tree that looked like Bb guns but you told us they were fishing poles. We did not believe that for one second lol I guess we were kinda spoiled. You were such an amazing person and had a pure soul. You could do no wrong in my eyes. And you definitely earned that.

I also remember my "Speeding Ticket" era lol because I had just started driving and I was so Impatient. I definitely wasn't going to tell you I had gotten like my 3rd ticket and I was broke lol but you found it in my car while you were using it. You initially told me that you did not have any money to spare and then you came back a day later and told me you would give me the money. I asked "how?" and you said that you would take it out of your light bill money. I said "and the lights?" to which you said you would be fine because you own the house and that was enough for you. But you had to know that I would not allow you to make that kind of sacrifice for my mistakes. So I told you no and that I would figure something out. To this day I have never felt more loved than I did that day. I wish I would have had the opportunity to share more of my life with you. So many conversions I want to have with you. Past and current. I could go on for days but I will wrap this up. I love you beyond measure and I miss you even more.

I often think that there must be a heaven, because I could not fathom the idea of never seeing you again. So until next time…

Dear, Nobody

I don't even know where to start. I thought I made peace with your passing a few months after. Maybe I did in some ways but It's true what they say, you never really "get over it" you just learn better ways to cope. I guess I should start from the beginning.

I walked onto the school campus in my favorite outfit, so I was in a good mood lol In the distance I heard someone say "There goes Johnny, we have to tell him." So they rushed up to me and said "Our friend is dead." In shock I stated "Huh" as if my ears were playing tricks on me. She repeated

"Our friend is dead, he was in a bad accident." I immediately felt my heart fall to my feet. Similar to a high "drop" on a roller coaster. I then went over to a mutual friend to confirm the news that I had just received. He assured me that nothing had been confirmed as of yet. In that moment I grasped on to that piece of hope as if my life depended on it.

We then went to class and waited anxiously. The principal came over the intercom and said that he had received reliable information and had the names of the individuals who had passed that morning. He said your name. My heart was back at my feet. I was speechless. Classmates asking me if I was ok. The teachers informed us that the school had brought in counselors and If we'd like to go see one we could. I declined.
I didn't know anything about the counseling process, grief or the long term effect of

trauma. Because speaking for myself, I'm sure I would have benefited from it. No one ever explained death or grief to me and that made it so much harder. Is still making it so much harder I feel. Had someone been around to say " counseling isn't a bad thing, you just have to find the right counselor" I would have been more open to the idea. Had someone said "I'll go with you." I would have been more open to the idea. Had someone said something.

This was on April 4th, and the candle light was on April 8th. On my birthday. Imagine that. That day I went to school, barely said a word to anyone. Right after I rode with some friends to your candlelight. It was obviously emotional and still overwhelming at that point. But I wasn't going to miss it. After that I went home and went straight to bed. I needed a break from reality.

For months after I was trying to process the grief I was feeling. Being Depressed and crying alone was the new normal for me. I was praying for closure, understanding and to get to talk to you one last time.

Eventually you did visit me in a dream, we sat on the bus bench outside of Howard and talked. I always thought that was an odd place but now I'm realizing that that's where we met. Interesting. I don't remember all of the details but I remember the key point which was you assuring me that you were ok and we had a few laughs. I woke up feeling a little better. I was able to smile. I did feel a weight being lifted off of my shoulders. That was the closure I needed at that time. But unfortunately the wound will never heal, not truly.

For a while I just tried not to think about it, because If I didn't think about it I couldn't be sad about it. Just me avoiding my grief.

Lol I was tired of being sad all the time. I also had a friend die a year before that, and another a year before that. Like, that was a lot. I was still a kid trying to process all of this on my own. I didn't really have anyone to talk to,
 not really. They either didn't understand or didn't care.

I remember trying to get you to come back to my school. I told you to tell your parents that I would come pick you up everyday since I was driving now and it was out of the bus district. lol We were always a powerhouse in basketball together when we played in the neighborhood. They always assumed I picked you because you were good, but it wasn't just that, we understood each other's playing style and strengths and we used that to our advantage. When you don't have strong relationships within your family you create those bonds with your friends. You are my brother and losing you was no different than losing a blood sibling. It changed me. In life you have "Pain points", moments that change your life forever. You were my first pain point. I'm sure you know but I still come visit your gravesite as often as I can handle & and I still go down that road where we had your candlelight.

I just want to make sure that you know I love you bro, I miss you and I'll never forget all of the memories we share. I wish I still had that video of us in your garage making up that dance routine. Good times man. I would give anything to relive those memories one more time. To just kick it and let the day get away from us like we did as kids.

I wasn't ready to lose you. But truthfully I never would have been so I guess that's why things happen on god's time and not mine lol rest in paradise my brother. I'll see you when I see you.

Dear, Nobody

I'll try not to make this too long incase you ever actually read it. Hell, I don't even know where to start. So much time has passed….We ran into each other a couple months ago at a gas station. It was very brief. Probably mostly due to me. Lol running into you honestly caught me off guard. I didn't know what to say. I know that sounds childish but it's the truth. We haven't really spoken in years. So I guess I just didn't know what we would talk about. I just know that I hate the fact that we haven't really spoken. I've thought many times about reaching out but I was never sure if you even would want me to. I know we had

our disagreements but we would always find our way back.
The last time you did try to reconnect and I was an asshole to you. I apologize for that. I wasn't in a good headspace then. I was dealing with a lot and I'm not using that as an excuse because that doesn't change what happened or how it must have made you feel which is why you stop trying.

After that you left for a while and we lost contact. Or stopped making an effort to remain in contact. Now we are a lot older and have our own lives that we have built without each other. I'm not saying we have to up each other's ass (no pun intended lol) but I would like to have my brother back. I'm sure I've already missed so much. I don't want to miss your wedding, the birth of your first kid or any other milestones in your life.

I know you don't like small talk so I will save you the trip down memory because we've

been through alot, I mean you were there.
Lol

So long story short, despite how much time has passed I miss my brother and if you are open to it we need to link and catch up.

Dear, Nobody

When we first met I thought you were so perfect for me. You had "The look", you said all the right things, did all the right things. It felt magical, even though we were in 2 different states. We spent most of the day on video chat, texting and sending photos of how our day was going. We even started sending letters and items so that we would feel closer to one another. Everything was perfect. Probably because we were still in the friend stage and there was no pressure.

You drove 16 hours to come stay with me for a week. And while you were here you asked me to be your boyfriend. I still remember how nervous you were. It was cute.

We had a pretty amazing week. We were both sad when you had to leave. But I think after that everything started to decline. We started to argue about who was moving where and when!? And that negative energy seemed to linger and intrude on other areas of our relationship. So eventually you moved here and things seem to have escalated because you expressed that you felt rushed. Which I think I understand a little better now. Seeing you stressed out about school and finding a decent job.

Not long after, you proposed for the second time. Because you proposed prior over the phone. You did it on the beach and asked to use my phone and went on my facebook live so all of my friends didn't miss it. It was cute. But I think that added more pressure lol I was excited and was like when are we getting married? You wanted to wait but I kept saying If we are sure we want to be together and we aren't going to walk away then why wait!? I was very oblivious to what marriage and living with another human entailed. This was my first adult relationship. I guess I can agree that I should have listened more.

So after my persistence we decided to get married. We go to the courthouse and get the paperwork. I found a cheap notary. So the ceremony was already off to a bad start, not professional at all. I honestly don't know why I went through with it. You definitely weren't feeling it. But I was young and wanted so badly to be married to the guy I was in love with. In my defense I honestly had good intentions when making that decision.

So we moved into a bigger apartment and filled it with everything we felt that we needed. Furniture, food, pets, misc. Items. But It didn't feel like a home for long. It began to feel like we were just roommates.we were still arguing about everything; From household rules, to bills, to my friends or your friends. Seemed like it was always something. A simple conversation about how our day was going would turn into an argument.

There are so many little details that come to mind but I'm not here to make anyone out to be a villain because there is always at least 2 sides to every story. You made it very clear after the separation that I was the villain. Lol The reality of it is we both contributed to a hostile living environment and we were hurting each other by staying together. There were obviously good times but it didn't outweigh the bad, for me. I even suggested an annulment as a solution to give us a reset and a chance to really enjoy the dating

stage. You took that as I didn't want to be with you anymore but I was just offering solutions. But I can see how that would make someone uneasy. Especially when I was the one who was rushing in the first place.
The more I think about it maybe you aren't as crazy as you seemed lol (laugh)

 I remember we were riding in the car together. Pretty sure we had argued that day. We could never disagree and let it go. We always carried it with us for the rest of the day or longer. But Sam smith - Too Good at Goodbyes came on the radio (which ironically just started playing) and we both were singing that song with broken hearts.

That was when I knew that things were taking a turn for the worst. And just as expected things progressively got worse. I stopped arguing. You made a statement that

I'll never forget. You said "Talking to you is like talking to a brick wall" That actually hurt my feelings. Because I just wasn't in a place where I knew how to communicate my feelings or be more assertive when speaking. So I would just let you rant, vent etc. The crazy thing is when we actually listened to each other instead of arguing we could communicate what was wrong and what needed to change for us to work but I think we had already checked out at that point because nothing seemed to change on either end. I also realized that I expected change in an unrealistic time frame. Especially since I hadn't changed either.
I later realized that I didn't always make the best decisions when it came to us. I didn't give you some of the courtesies that I was expecting. It got to a point where we didn't make sense anymore so I made another decision for the both of us. It wasn't easy.

My intention was never to hurt you. I just needed to stop hurting myself. That choice was for both of us.

When we first met and we were talking about goals and dreams I told you that I will always want you to be happy, even if it wasn't with me....

Dear, Nobody

Despite whatever image of me you have created in your head, I'm not perfect. I have been through so much and I'm still working through some of it. I have come a long way with hard work and dedication. I face things head on when I'm ready to face them. I have a big heart but once you abuse it you will never get that same heart again. I do not hold grudges but I do not forget either. We all have a pass. I'm always open to talking about it if asked genuinely.

If you ask around about me some people will say I'm the sweetest guy they've ever met, others will say I'm a b***ch.

Believe them all. I reciprocate energy. Treat me how you want to be treated. The few people that truly know me will probably say I'm a handful; But I'm worth it. Lol I inherited a short temper and smart mouth, just a heads up lol I mean no harm. Unless I'm reciprocating energy lol

In all seriousness, I'm genuinely a nice guy. I like basketball, Roller Skating, Intimate walks, Movie nights (I'm going to fall asleep though) trying new food, and my all time favorite, anything with the right people. I'm afraid of heights but It doesn't stop me from doing height sensitive activities. I'm planning to go skydiving but If I haven't gone by the time we meet you should take me lol I won't go alone. I'm also afraid of the ocean. Self explanatory. And no, I can't. I have big dreams and aspirations but I really enjoy the simple things life has to offer.

I still enjoy Disney movies and music. I'm still a Hannah Montana fan. I like small reptiles, and alligators lol At first sight you're going to think I'm this rough guy who may not have much going on but most of the time I'm a teddy bear who just wants to be surrounded by the people he cares about the most. It's actually not that complicated lol

But Patience is a virtue ;P

Dear, Nobody

You have to forgive yourself the same way you forgive others. It's ok. You are ok. You were not designed to be perfect. S**t happens. And it's not always happening to you, sometimes it happens for you. Everything happens for a reason. You can't control everything. You were dealt a hand and now you have to play with it. And you have to admit. As bad as you think this hand is, you have been executing consistently with it. Because of it. Everything you went through taught you a lesson that you needed to get to the next level. Kinda like an escape room. So stop counting your losses and count your wins. Stop acting like God made a mistake when he created you. It's disrespectful. You're doing the work and you're getting better everyday. Why don't you feel like you deserve a seat at the table? Why are you hiding from the world when you know god put something inside of you that the world needs otherwise he wouldn't have needed you. You have a purpose. Own it. Acknowledge it. Walk in it. Don't ever let anyone make you feel inadequate. You are created in the image of the lord. You are royalty. Now stop playing games and go and get what god has ordained for you. No one else can claim it but you.

You are the chosen one!

Dear, Reader

First and foremost, thank you for taking the time to read this book and embrace my journey with me. I truly appreciate you and everything you do in support of my brand. <3

Don't take this the wrong way but I don't care what you went through or are going through because this is only a season, it is not your whole life nor does it single handedly define who you are. You will overcome and you will be more resilient, more intelligent and more prepared for what god has planned next for you. Life isn't easy for anyone, yet the world is overpopulated. That means people are finding ways to overcome it.

And they are human just like you, I am human just like you. If I can do it there is no reason you can't. I don't want to hear the reason why you think you can't, tell me the reasons you think you can. Always speak positivity and prosperity over your life, dreams and goals. You have to manifest the things that you desire. Say it out loud everyday all day. Say it until you believe it. Write it down. Write it 100 times like the teachers used to make us do. They did that because the more you write it the more you read it and the more you instill it in your brain that this will come to fruition. They had us manifesting "I will not talk in class" lol wild. But see how things come full circle. All the answers you need are either already in you or near you. You just have to manifest them.

And if you would like to receive this healing and motivating energy every morning then take out your phone right now, text "Motivate" to 352-290-8759.

I offer accountability coaching and 1 on 1 personal development as well. The best part is, it's all free for a limited time.

So don't waste anymore time. Let's get you to the next level so you can live your best life.

Let's reflect

 Do any of these letters make you think of anyone that you want to write a letter to? It's ok, It's a part of the process. This is how we get to the other side of the anger, the anxiety and the depression. Take your time, there is no rush.

This is a 3 part exercise.

Part 1 - The letter

Part 2 - Feeling and processing

Part 3 - Releasing

Are you ready?

Dear, Nobody

Processing

Take a second to breathe. You did it! You completed your first letter. I'm Proud of you. Honestly. It's never easy facing these parts of us that we have buried for so long. Simply to feel normal, to avoid not truly being heard, to have a moment to just be. I totally get it. That's why I'm so proud of you.

Give me 3 words to describe how you feel right now.

1.________________________________

2.________________________________

3.________________________________

Now I want you to think about why you feel that way.

Let's talk about how you're going to take control of how this affects you. What can you do to ensure peace in mind, body and spirit?

Release

This can be done in a number of different ways. If you have one that resonates more with you then do it your way.

Option 1 - tear the letter from the book and burn it. Say your goodbyes and Release all that negative energy associated with that letter and let go of all those burdens and emotions that you have curried for far too long. Take your power back.

Option 2 - Tear the letter from the book, fold it and hole punch it. Tie it to a helium balloon. Say your goodbyes and Release all that negative energy associated with that letter and let go of all those burdens and emotions that you have curried for far too long. Take your power back.

Take a little more time to feel and just be.

We are almost done

What is next for you?

This process can be very draining. So if you need more time to complete this step I totally understand. Just don't wait too long. Don't get scared or discouraged. You just climbed a major hill that most people are still too afraid to climb. You have to Acknowledge that you may be stronger than you thought. *smiley face*
If you get through this you can get through anything. Life is about having a strong mind more than anything. Mental toughness is the true secret. Because if you can just keep going eventually you will get there. That's a fact. Take you back to the story we heard as kids about the turtle and the rabbit. Consistency wins the race. Never forget that. And as i've stated. I'm always here if you want a second opinion or just need a bit of motivation. We are family now. I got you.

So, what is next for you?

Your Safe Space

www.ingramcontent.com/pod-product-compliance
Lightning Source LLC
Chambersburg PA
CBHW070730011025
33374CB00090B/2375